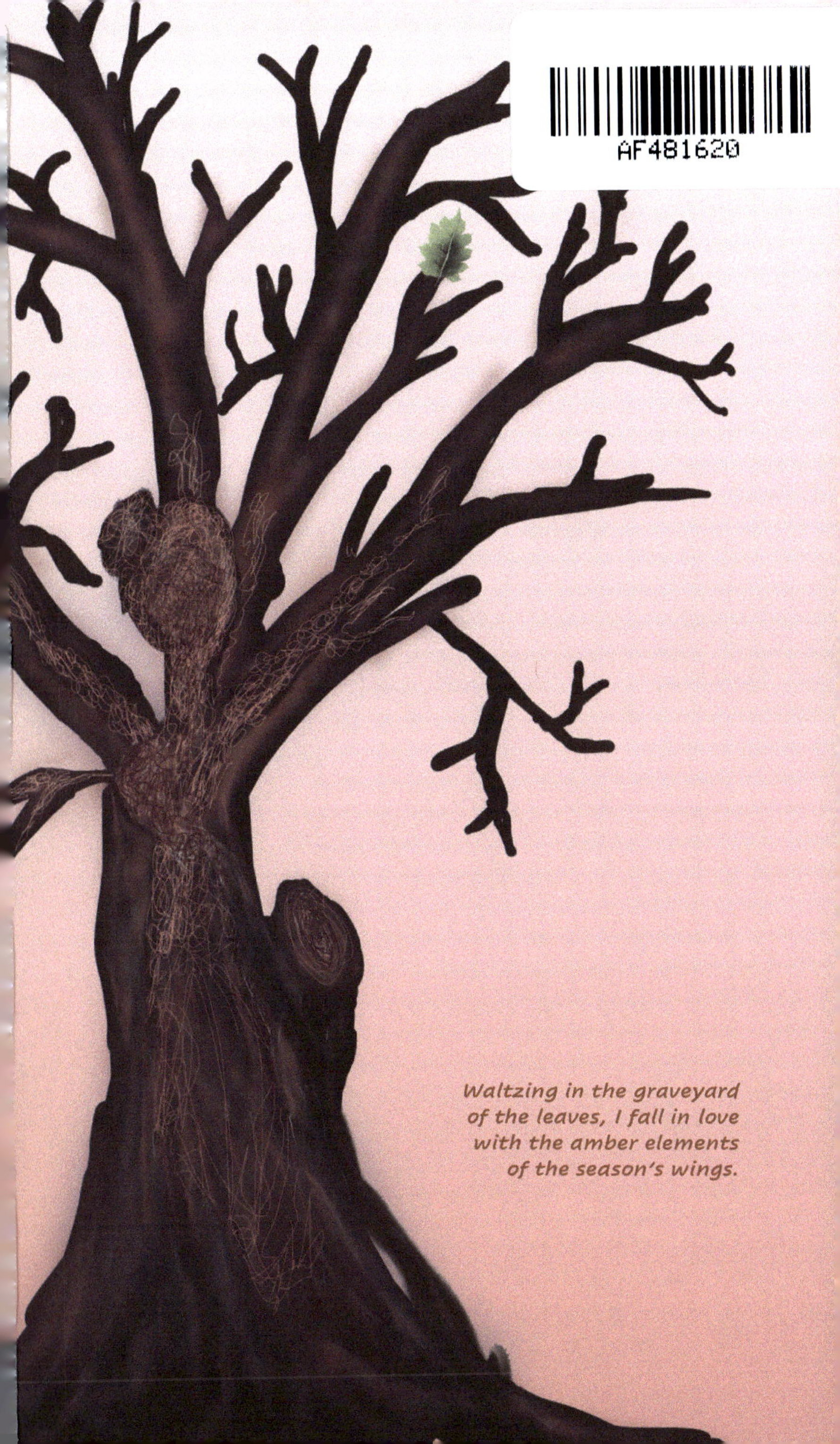

AF481620
Waltzing in the graveyard
of the leaves, I fall in love
with the amber elements
of the season's wings.

Solo Works

To read more about Reena Doss' other published works,
visit her website at www.reenadoss.com

Pearl On A Summer Leaf

An autobiographical collection

Swallowing The Moon

Ballads from my heart

The Story Of 8

13 Reasons Why I Choose Love

The Last Leaf Of

AUTUMN

Barefoot and falling,
infinity is a number that has none to end

REENA DOSS

Ink Gladiators Press® Publication

First Edition
Copyright © 2023 Reena Doss

The Last Leaf Of Autumn

Barefoot and falling, infinity is a number that has none to end

ISBN 13: 978-93-90766-68-0

Developmental Editing:
Miriam Otto @miriamo77

Copyediting & Proofing:
Shruti Sharma @shrutiscapes

Cover, Book Design & Illustrations:
Leonie Belle Hawk @leoniebellehawk

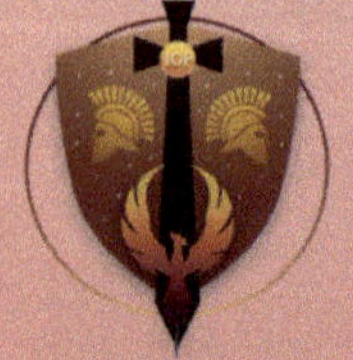

Ink Gladiators Press®
Publishing and promoting warriors on life's battlefield

Founded in 2019 | Bangalore 560077, India
www.inkgladiatorspress.com

Dedication
A season within a lifetime

Thank you to my beloved Weaver—Creator of every being and generation, the night and the day, the inhale and exhale of seasons, life and death, loved ones and lost ones, the trees and leaves, the love of my life and me.

This book is dedicated to the friend I never expected to receive—Miriam Otto. Thank you for helping me unleash the stories that needed to spill from the ink in my heart.

May this labor of love find all those who adore Autumn's fire of colors as much as I do.

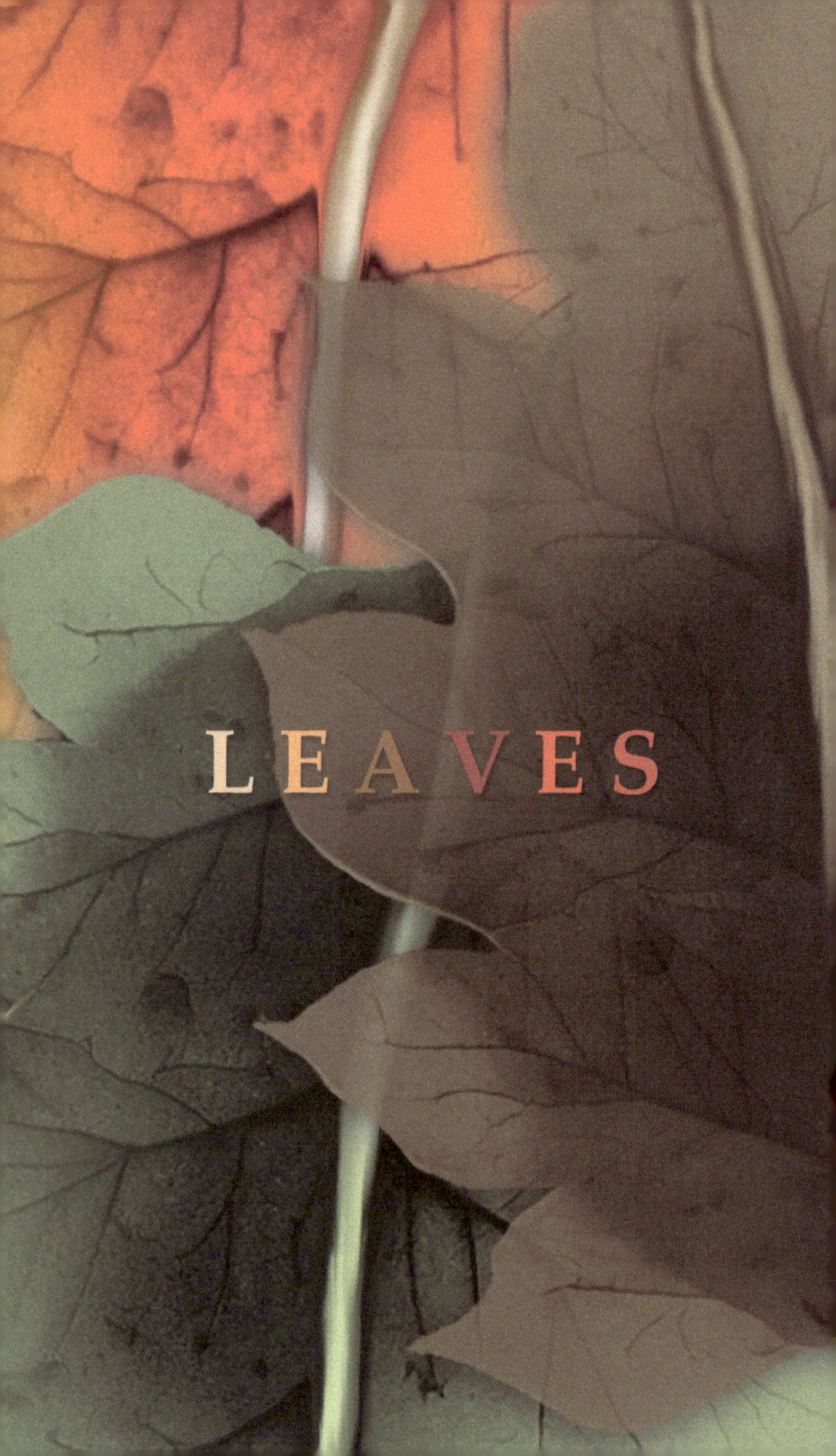
LEAVES

Letter from the Author

Dear Reader,

If you have decided to pick this book from my library heart, then allow me to welcome you warmly to this hearth. In my stories, there is always a lit fireplace with the most beautiful embers for all those who need a safe place to feel, to dream and to hope. Let me find you in the places where you have known sorrow, failure and experienced the heaviness of being at the receiving end of injustice.

A moon heart has many scars and every one of them is extremely important because they lead to a voice that couldn't be heard by those you loved. Learn with me here how to find the best pieces of yourself in every chapter of this story. There will be pieces that you know can no longer be. There will also be pieces that others stuck into you that you know do not belong anymore. This will be more tough to let go (because you might have mistaken them as part of you) but when you do, you will find that the places or voids left underneath those wounds will get shaped into a foundation ready for the most transformative stars to emerge. Then will you know how to create them.

I feel what I have not yet experienced but will go through and I share it not for myself alone but for all those on the same path of growth. To understand this is to know that this is sometimes the curse and blessing of being an old soul.

I promise there will be storms that make you want to give up. There will be rain which will feel unending. There will be a time when listening grows more within you. There will be a purpose for all of it. There will be a time for acceptance. Then there will be a death that feels like falling into the abyss before you step into the joy of many lovely beginnings.

Reconcile with these truths and know that it is your own voices that also feel the unaccustomed need and right to bloom in you. You are YOU—a season of many—all tied together and beautiful in all your past versions that were trying their best to bloom. You were made to live with the courage of grace, not pride.

It is okay to not be busy so you can discover its blessings. You were made for a purpose to move, not stay stuck. It is okay to rest in the new. You were made to be more, not less. It is okay to inject all these big thoughts into the ink of your heart as gently or as fiercely as you need.

Let yourself be inspired. Make creations that will move other hearts.

May my quill of Hope always find you in the dark!

Reena Doss

Dated till Autumn no longer exists.

For *the love of my life*

Dearest,

You were sent as hope to enter the soil of ashes within my metaphorical versions of death.

Thank you for walking with me every single day during these five years, no matter the miles. Thank you for standing by me and standing up to me throughout all my seasons of doubt. Thank you for not just believing in my dreams but joining in... in everything that I undertook on this new path without hesitation but with arms wide open and in enthusiasm. You were courageous to enter a tornado of storms—that didn't know it was more than one—and to hold them until they discovered that what lay beneath the void of grief carried only Love. How could I ever forget someone like you?

You deserve a lifelong harvest of golden leaves wherever you go in life.

With Love always,
Starlight

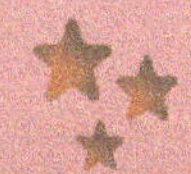

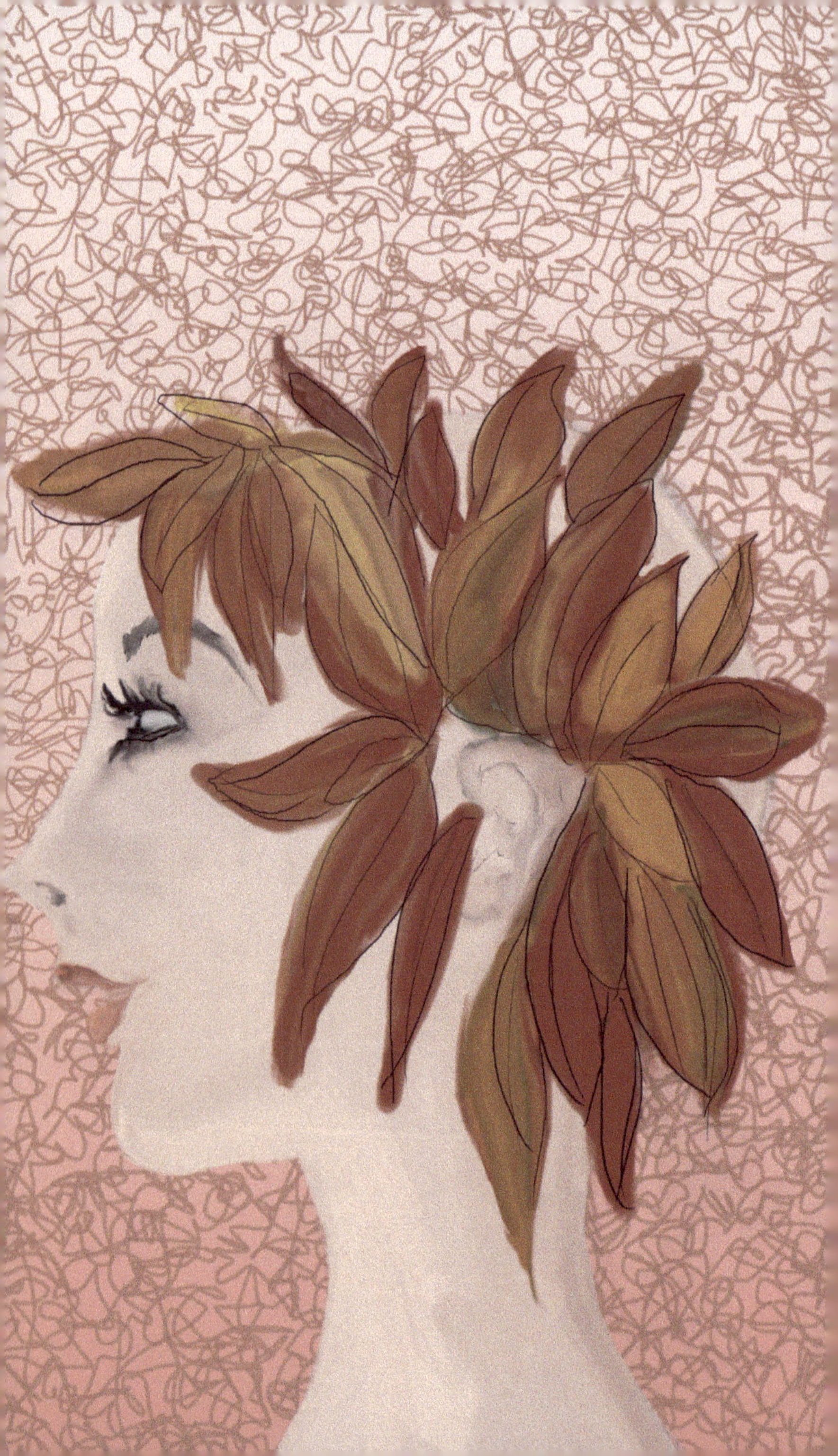

Table Of Contents

Barefoot and falling, infinity is a number that has none to end

*I stopped numbering my pages. Infinity seems to be a better number
and my story is still unwritten. Besides, I do like its symbol a lot—
a sleeping ∞*

A Map Of Seasons

Find me in the depths of you, constant
in my never changing essence but always transforming self.

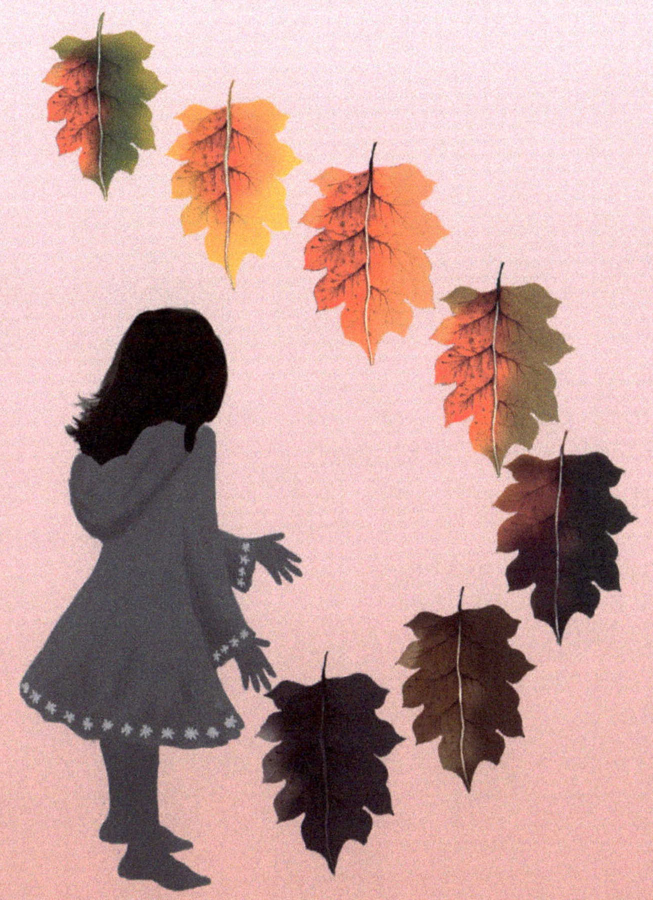

The Last Leaf Of Autumn

∞

When I spend time with children, I learn how to be my best self but I also don't forget that this was a phase in my life where I learned how to be afraid. I developed protective layers that sometimes hindered me from doing things that I know I could do but didn't.

Sometimes, humanity breaks my heart, when I observe the choices they make during hard times. It is complicated to decipher what I don't myself know about, yet it is also easy to be compassionate about the things I hold in mystery. In those moments, I can't help wondering how different intensities were reached in situations that affected decision-making based on the history of how every life moved, moves and will move upon the face of the Earth.

As I stepped back into the world with new grace after healing things I sometimes did not get a chance to talk about, though I yearned to, I learned slowly and fast how people are either processing pain, healing from it or choosing to be the very hands of cruelty that they did not imagine becoming. This is why I began to dedicate time in trying to understand my roots, healing from what broke me down as I found the courage to pour fresh water into the eroded areas where salt got too absorbed in their textures to flush out what shouldn't stay. Sometimes, I have had to cut the rotten ones out, lift the roots that had hidden for too long into the sunlight as well as address some heavy ones with my voices of creative expression to feel the relief in letting something new grow from them.

Pause with me here. Exhale deeply.

It is challenging learning how to turn into a new leaf but it isn't impossible… if you do it one step at a time—by yourself, with those you love or maybe with this little book (which is a piece of me that I gift gladly to you). You are wanted, needed and important in this life. That's what matters. That's why you were created. You.

May I suggest that you add compassion, empathy and love to the answers you give to the questions you ask yourself as you turn each page? Can you say "No" when you cannot commit to something? Can you speak up when you need space and know your limitations? Can you do this, especially during healing times?

Discernment is important when navigating through a reality that often concludes that those who are choosing to be kind are either too much, too naïve or too sweet. You deserve the good things in life and therefore, you must remember that this is what you need to affirm to the future of a self you are developing into.

Don't be afraid to meet, grieve and then let go of those memories, things and people that have intentionally and unintentionally torn you in places you wish you hadn't been. Make sure you are fair in this as no one is perfect, including yourself.

After all, *we* are a map of seasons—always Summer, Spring, Monsoon, Autumn, Winter, You and I.

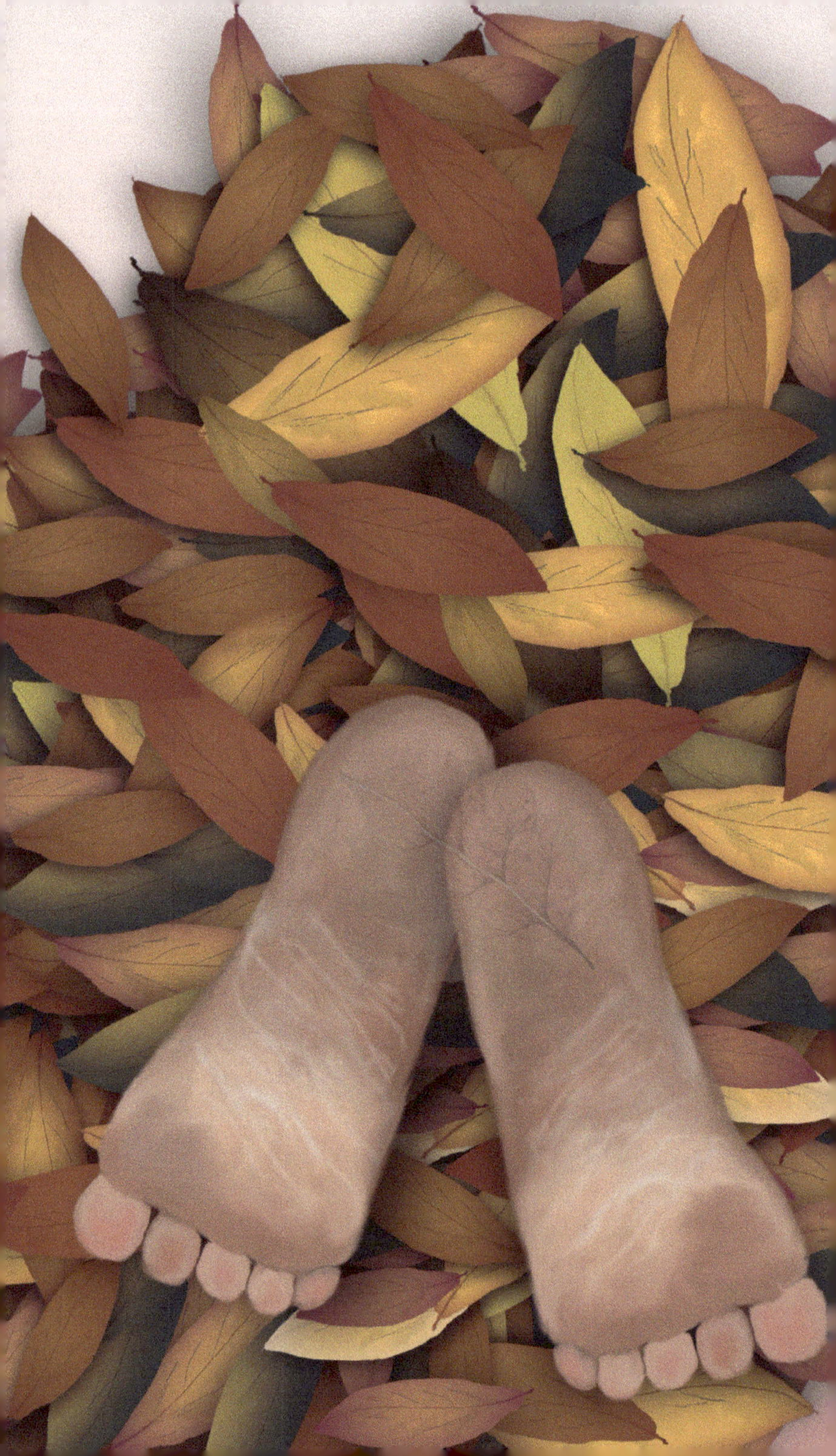

Barefoot

*I kick off sandals and feel
the wet mud under my feet…
I want to taste everything about Autumn
when I am footloose.*

Letting go of a situation, a person or thing can be an incredibly tough decision.

After a long period of false starts, some people need a split second to take a chance on moving forward. There are some who will allow a decision to lead them when they are ready but there are also a few who struggle with change, terrified it will dip them into something worse than where they came from.

However, the truth—as the Last Leaf in Autumn finds out to his surprise—is that there is no joy in holding on or feeling stuck in a situation that has become too painful to stay in. Life is and will always be about change. Moving into the next chapter of your story is a very natural part of growing up and learning who you can be.

Never forget: Something better will certainly come around the corner after you have gone through all the tests that adversity provides.

*I am a part of the Earth, ocean wild
and always falling like the waves do for the shore.*

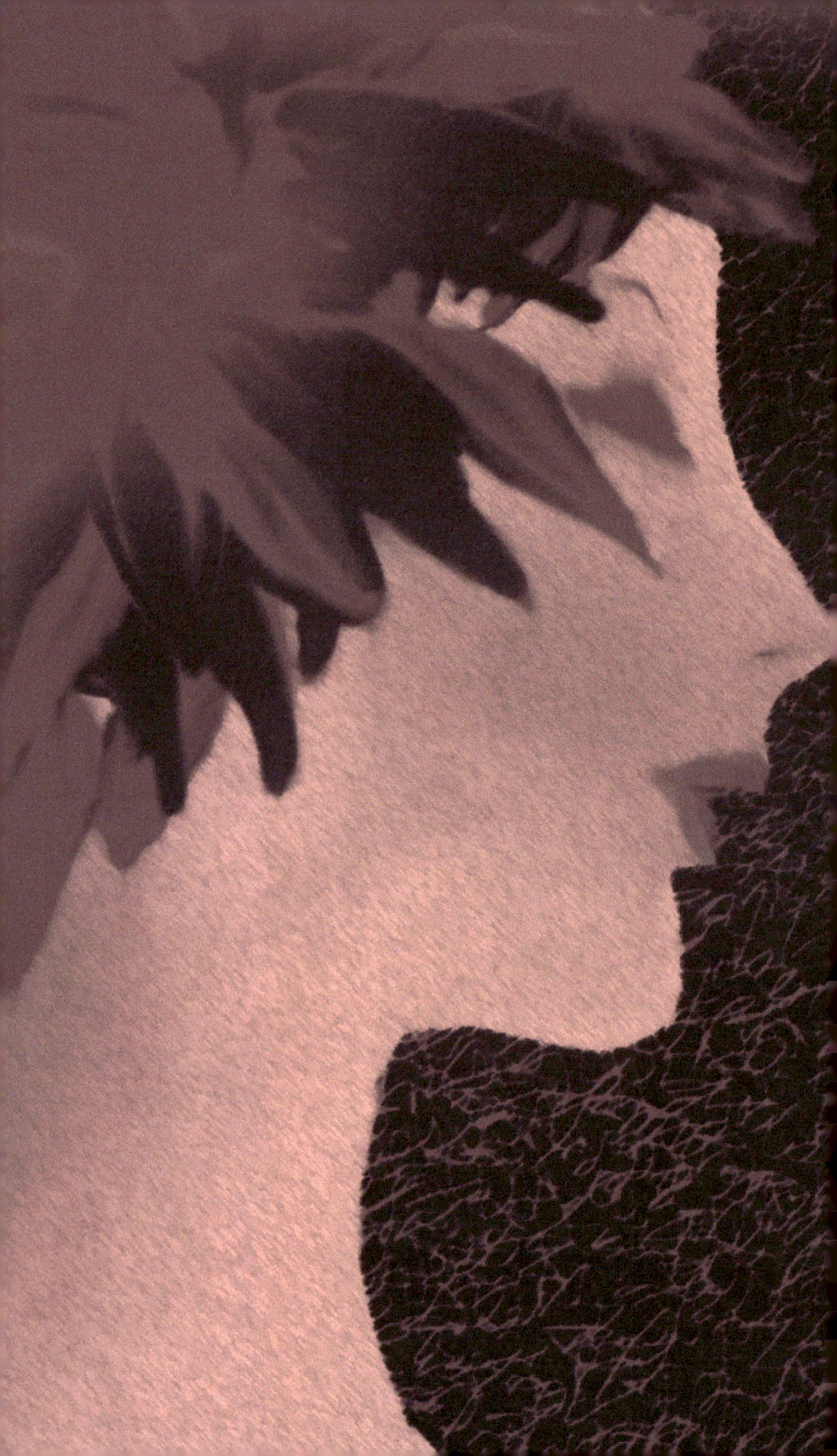

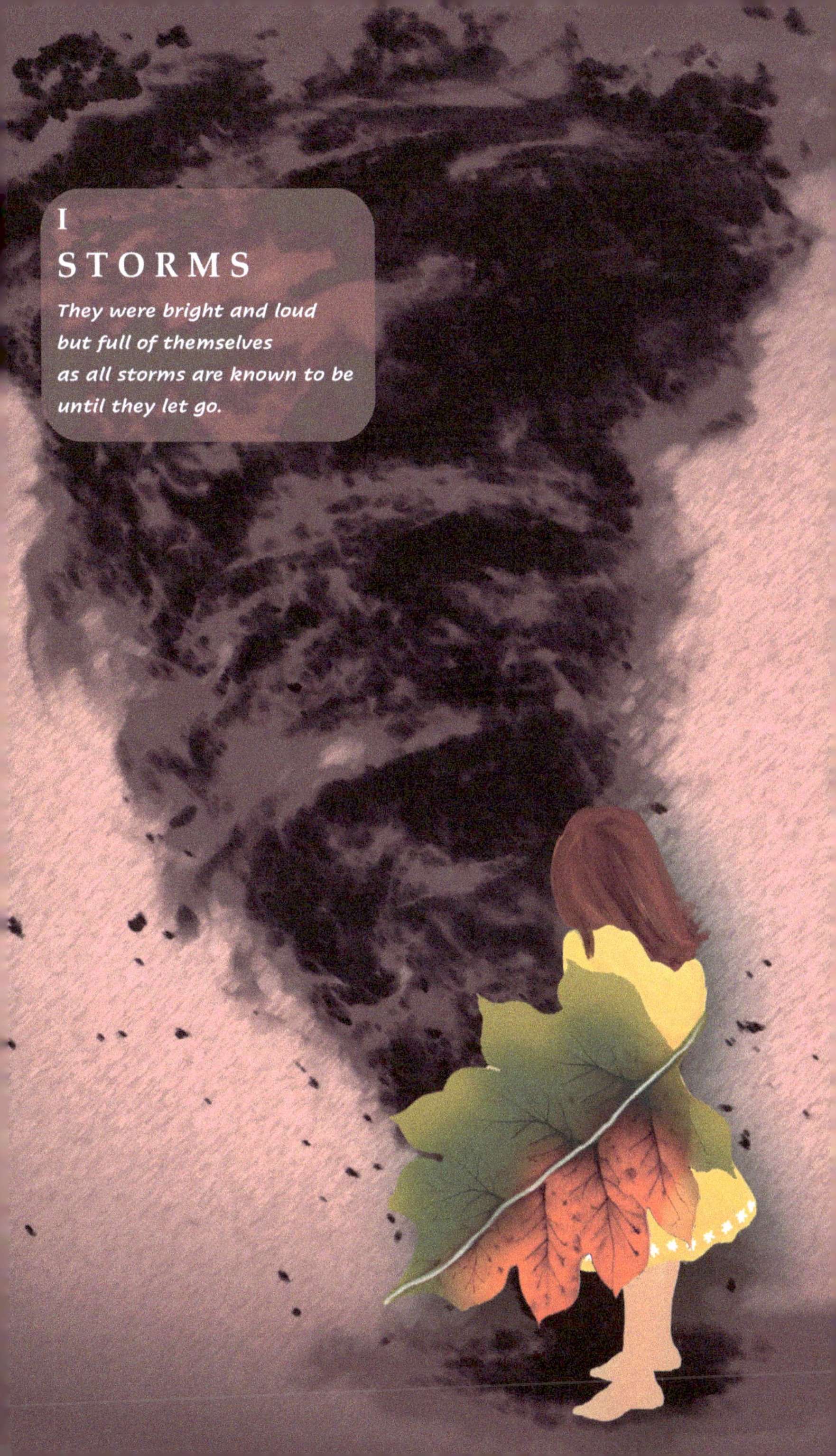

I
STORMS
They were bright and loud
but full of themselves
as all storms are known to be
until they let go.

I was uncomfortable with Autumn.

I knew a lot about the fall
from high branches to lowly places,
the dying of glorious days
to forgotten, cold memories
and the stillness of old bones
to rotting, strangling decay.

I was happy holding on.

Life was monotonous
but I was still here,
alive and breathing under the stars
with the Tree that gave me all I needed.

I was still green but wise enough
to refuse to spread open
the folds in my leaf.

I was happy holding on,
wasn't I?

Barefoot and falling, infinity is a number that has none to end

I was not going to allow the Sun
to paint in its prettiest colors.

Doing so
would seal my fate like the rest.

But that's the way life worked,
didn't it?

Everyone did it—
living for something greater than themselves
but I, I would choose to live
for myself.

Who could stop
and tell me otherwise?

It was mine to live
in the way I chose.

Reena Doss

I woke up to the falling leaves,
as they left the branches of the Tree
that we had been attached to.

Where were they going?
Why did they choose to leave?

I didn't like that they left me alone,
clinging to the life I was given.

They called out joyfully
as they crumbled to the ground,
inviting me to be
a part of something I didn't know
and that they couldn't explain
adequately enough.

"Marvelous and beautiful", they said,
"This glorious ecstasy,
this falling
into the unknown mystery
is also your marked
destiny."

Reena Doss

Barefoot and falling, infinity is a number that has none to end

I thought they looked disgusting,
rotting and blending in with the Earth
while the wind carried others to places
I didn't think
I would like to know about.

Where was the glory of falling?

It was stupid to grow old
and die in such a horrible way.

They didn't fight at all
as they slept through the storms,
got stuck within hurricanes,
drowned in tsunamis,
allowing themselves to tremble wildly
with the earthquakes.

The Last Leaf Of Autumn

∞

I held tight and stayed vigilant
until a day came by
to shatter my comfort zone.

My Autumn came in the shape of a girl
who used to visit my beloved Tree.

Barefoot and falling, infinity is a number that has none to end

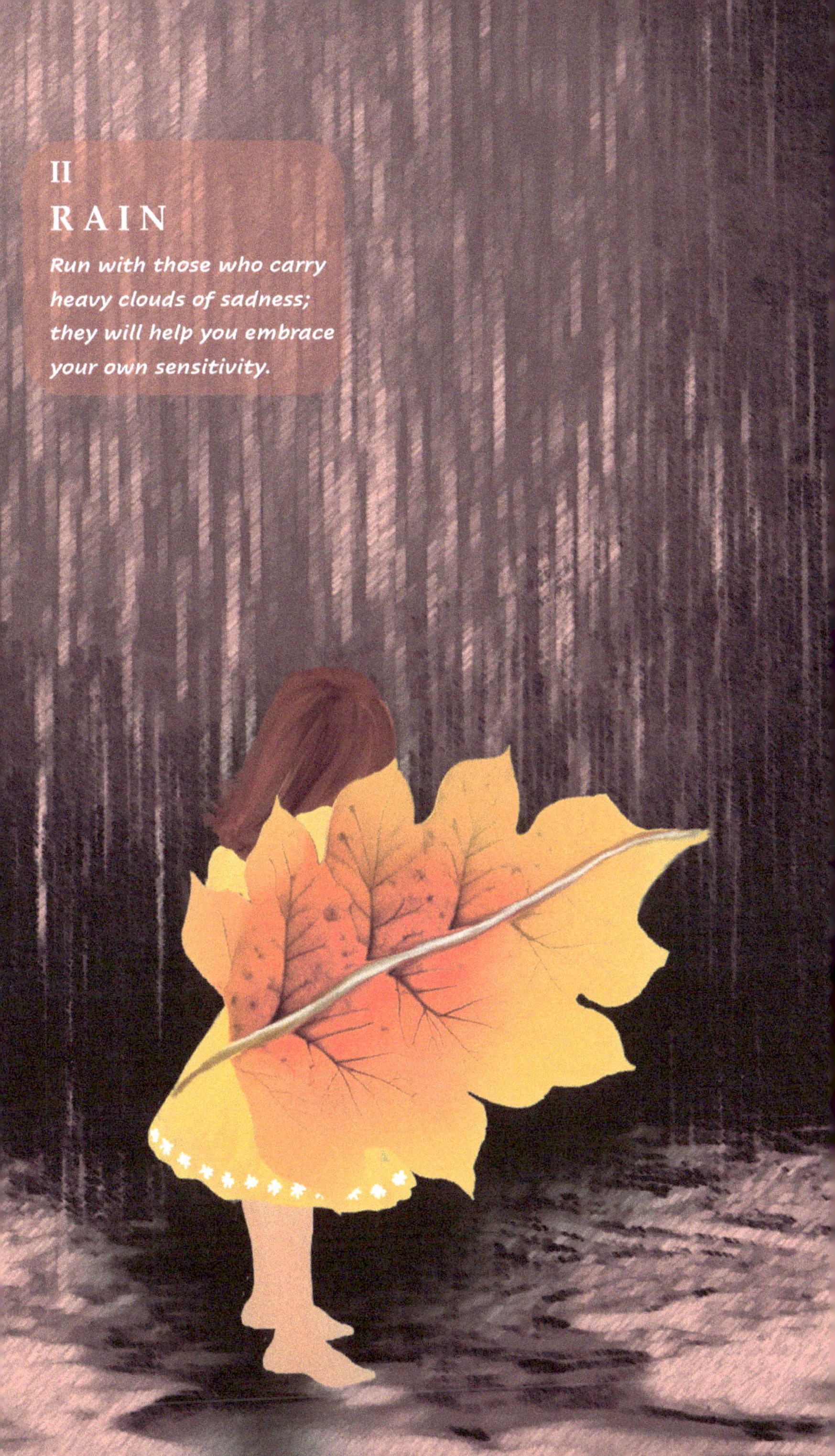

II
RAIN

Run with those who carry
heavy clouds of sadness;
they will help you embrace
your own sensitivity.

The Girl would lean against its trunk
to speak softly, melodiously sweet,
often appreciating the listening silence
as my siblings rustled excitedly, swaying…
trying to answer those questions she had
though she never heard a word they said.

I never heard my Tree speak with her
so I didn't talk either.

What was the point anyway?
It's not like she could hear me.
Besides, would she want to listen?

She seemed too grown up for her age
Why didn't she enjoy herself more?

Today, the sky was moody.

I observed everyone scurry around,
desperate to be back home safe and dry
before the wet showers drenched them all.

I wasn't happy with my current situation.

My siblings, friends and all I had known
had been falling all day.

Reena Doss

That Girl in a yellow frock emerged suddenly,
making her way towards us,
looking more lost than usual.

I watched as the Girl ran,
blinded by her own misery,
trampling over my brethren,
barefooted,
bleeding
and talking to herself.

Barefoot and falling, infinity is a number that has none to end

Thunder crackled and lightning struck—
hitting my Tree's imposing branches.

The rest of her leaves fell
under the twilight sky
leaving her…
empty and bereft of life.

A once formidable sight
when full of Spring and Summer,
she now stood alone,
barren and forsaken
with loyal me,
hugging her tightly.

The Girl was mumbling something.
It was hard to understand
what she said sometimes.

The rain and wind
beat her shuddering body,
soaking and mocking her futile efforts
to find shelter in the Tree's branches.

Barefoot and falling, infinity is a number that has none to end

She looked up as if to speak
like she had before
but saw just me
and for some reason,
she burst into tears.

I didn't understand why noticing me
would render such uncontrollable sobbing.

Something about her moved me
and I found myself asking,
"Why do you bring your sadness here?
Isn't it enough that you are free?"

Barefoot and falling, infinity is a number that has none to end

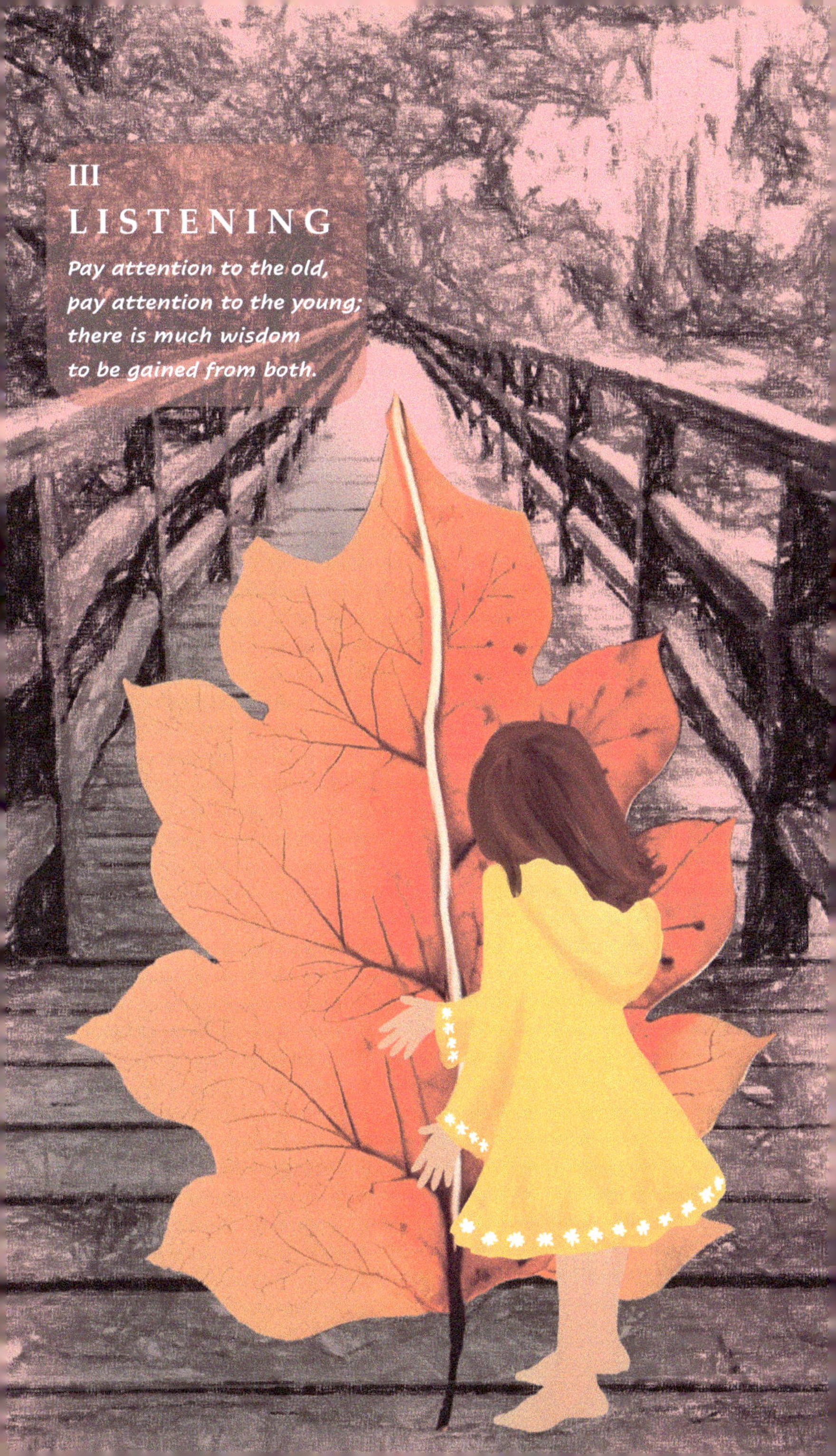

III
LISTENING
Pay attention to the old,
pay attention to the young;
there is much wisdom
to be gained from both.

Her eyes crisscrossed on hearing me,
wildly searching for its source,
but then looked flabbergasted
when she realized I had spoken.

"A talking leaf?"
she gasped, stunned.

I hadn't known humans could hear us
because she hadn't heard my family
when they had tried to speak to her.

I didn't respond right away.
I was trying to unravel answers
locked inside questions
that were flooding my brain.

I was unable to comprehend why
she could hear me speak.

"I guess I imagined it", she said,
rousing me from my slumber
of drifting thoughts.

"You didn't", I replied.
The question is… why?
I thought.

Barefoot and falling, infinity is a number that has none to end

She shrugged, easily accepting the fact
that this was a possibility,
while I grappled with fear,
confusion filtering through
like I was falling somewhere
in a place I didn't yet know—
that I had somehow
missed something vital.

The Last Leaf Of Autumn

∞

"I have something to reveal
yet I am uncertain of its meaning.
It plagues my heart's strings
and makes me walk like a day zombie",
she said.

"Nothing makes sense,
nothing bad happened
but home stopped being home
and yet it's all that has ever mattered."

"What do you mean?"
I asked her.

"Fall came after Spring
shocking my mind ruthlessly
that has always lived in daydreams",
she answered me, softly.

"I find that I am no longer content and happy
in the place I ran first to feel safe.
Does this mean I no longer care about
all the things that made me feel whole?"

Her voice had shifted to a deeply reflective tone
and I did not want to interrupt her
as I had become curious
about what she was talking about.

"I feel an overwhelming need
to search for a place
where surrender becomes possible",
she said.

I was about to tell her
I couldn't help
when I found myself pausing…

Barefoot and falling, infinity is a number that has none to end

Not everyone saw a leaf
and thought it had value.
She was unique.

I liked that she of all the visiting humans
found time to appreciate us,
though we were
a few among many.

I thought she had forgotten I was there
when she suddenly turned around
to directly ask me a question.

"Tell me, Little Leaf, how do you know
when home is no longer home,
when the things you've known forever
hurt you deep inside your soul?"

The rains had stopped by this time,
with the Earth plastering her feet in dirt.

Barefoot and falling, infinity is a number that has none to end

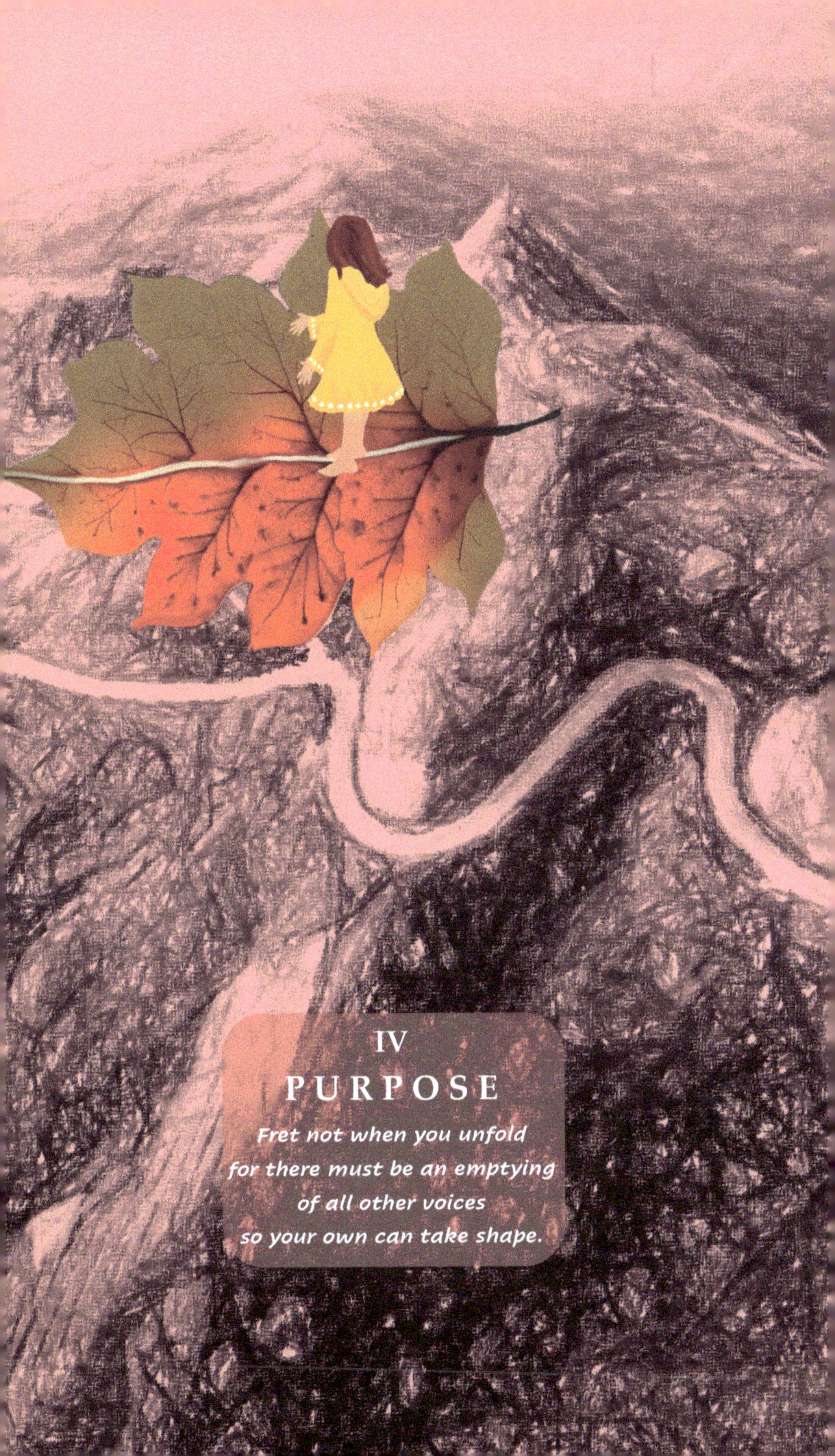
IV
PURPOSE
Fret not when you unfold
for there must be an emptying
of all other voices
so your own can take shape.

Reena Doss

Something powerful
was waking up within me.

I couldn't stop its magnetic pull,
no matter how much I tried
because this time—
I didn't want to.

I shook the droplets off my leaf,
spread open my folds,
to discover the russet red beauty
I hid from view.

My voice spoke words
I did not recognize.

"I'd like for this season to wrap me safe
'lest I fall but how can I know
where I'm supposed to be
if I hold on to fear, afraid of it all,
when the truth openly says,
I no longer belong."

I let out a sigh,
feeling an odd sense of peace
before I continued....

"So when your lungs press into you,
and the voice in your heart calls for change,
can you feel that choking strangling your insides
announcing your journey's end?

Then feel free to reshape yourself
into a better version for the coming times.

You were never meant to be caged.

I hope you search and acquire the courage
to discover who you are
because then will you realize
where you truly must be.

Though it maybe another temporary stay,
often, after the hard fall is accomplished,
you'll see another path that may or may not last.

And then life will be beautiful when you feel
untamed nature beat in your chest again."

I let go then
to show the Girl she could too.

I didn't know
I was capable of doing what I'd feared
and this rawest part of me
was bleeding from breaking away
from everything I had known.

But as I fell,
she caught me gently
to kiss the parts
that hurt the most.

Barefoot and falling, infinity is a number that has none to end

Afraid of the unknown,
we both were;
but understanding
that moving forward
meant creating space
for the new.

She set me down
upon the ground
with a kindness
rarely encountered.

Reena Doss

Perhaps dreams
could now become a reality?

It didn't seem right
that what we felt should stay
only in our minds.

They wanted to be born
and we wanted to be ready.

A cheery skip in her walk,
she left my side
off to beckoning adventures,
her arms open.

Barefoot and falling, infinity is a number that has none to end

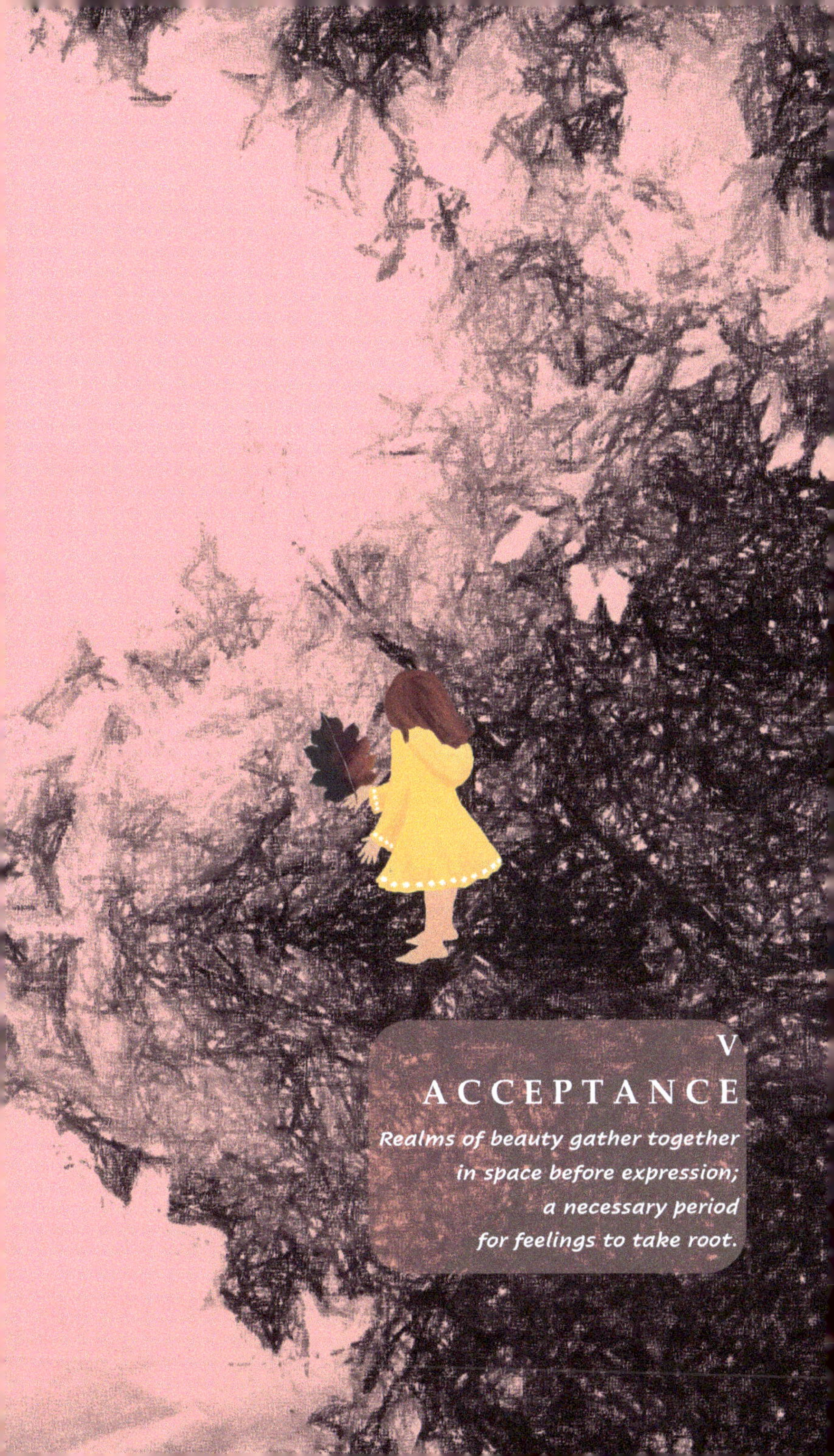

V
ACCEPTANCE
Realms of beauty gather together
in space before expression;
a necessary period
for feelings to take root.

Night was no more,
dying out to welcome
the skies' transformation;
a new story,
alightened with daybreak.

I lay in grateful acceptance
for my role in the Girl's story.

Yet I still couldn't stop the tremor
that passed through my veins
when I heard the laughter of children
running towards me where I lay.

I had, after all, fought till the end
with every fiber of my being.

I watched them chase each other over me,
another generation exactly like I had been.

Carelessly thinking, freely believing,
that they had all the time they wanted,
not realizing their purpose yet…
was to carve nations into existence
with what they would fight so hard against.

Yet, it felt right somehow
that they should be children now,
growing into their pain,
learning about their shadows
for it is in this heart wrenching agony,
that their truest bravest light will align
to reach out and touch other lives'.

I smiled…
It was a long, long time coming
but I finally understood
that my fears had been relevant
as they served to prepare me
for my unknown purpose
that I had resisted adamantly before.

Uncertain of why I was fulfilling it,
why I felt I had to care
about something I didn't want,
until I realized to my surprise
that it was all I ever wanted,
to acknowledge I had become ready
to partake of my permanent place.

I hadn't known that this Girl
was the one to tend to
my sowing in Winter,
my blooming in Spring,
my growing in Summer,
my healing in Monsoon
leading the way to embrace
the uncomfortable beautiful task
of making peace with Autumn.

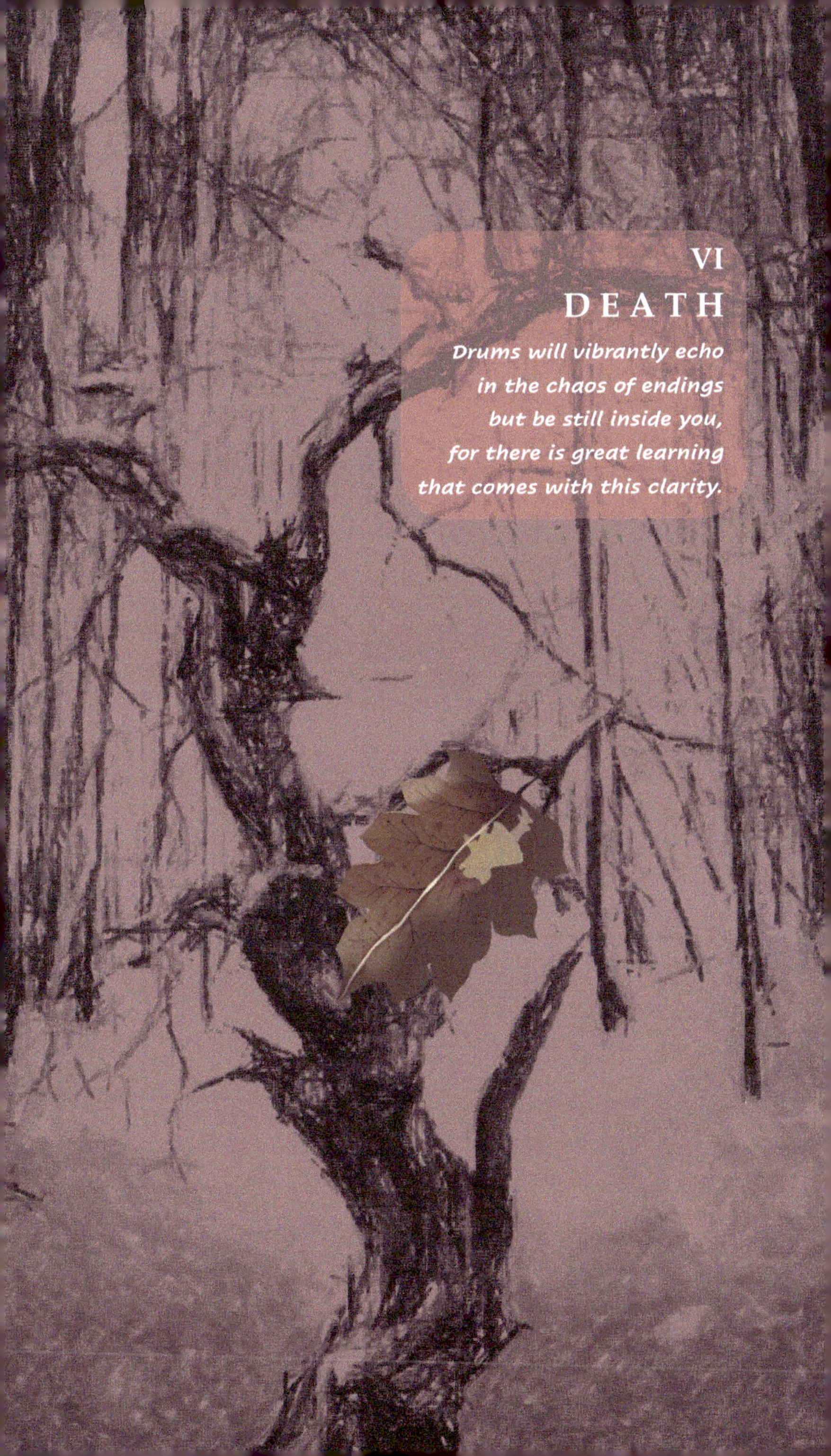

VI
DEATH
Drums will vibrantly echo
in the chaos of endings
but be still inside you,
for there is great learning
that comes with this clarity.

As I laid myself open
to their innocent naked feet,
I crumbled easily
knowing my destiny had been inevitable.

I welcomed the crushing,
the breaking and the helplessness
of my mortal state.

In that moment of total surrender,
I heard a gentle voice like a balm
from my Tree that did not speak before.

"Little Leaf, you were a gift
to the Girl, a story for the world
and will always be a part of me.
New leaves will grow in Spring
but not a single one can take your place
They will have their own
and must learn about their destiny."

Barefoot and falling, infinity is a number that has none to end

Her words of wisdom brought the wind
and it picked up my frail pieces,
tenderly lifting and carrying them away,
though one question surfaced
where I faltered between time.

"Mother", I asked my beloved Tree.
"Where oh where is the wind taking me?"

"To soften hard soil",
Mother replied,
"to bring life to the hopeless,
to whisper love in the ears of those
who think they are far too damaged,
to produce fruit in dark places,
where there is no faith in possible miracles
in their lifetime of tidal growth."

"And after that, where will I go?"
I asked out of curiosity,
fear far behind me now.

My Tree had no more leaves.
Our remnants were but dust
tucked into the freshly scented Earth.

"When it is time to say goodbye, Little Leaf
you will return to Him."
she said, her voice becoming faint,
almost fading away.

Barefoot and falling, infinity is a number that has none to end

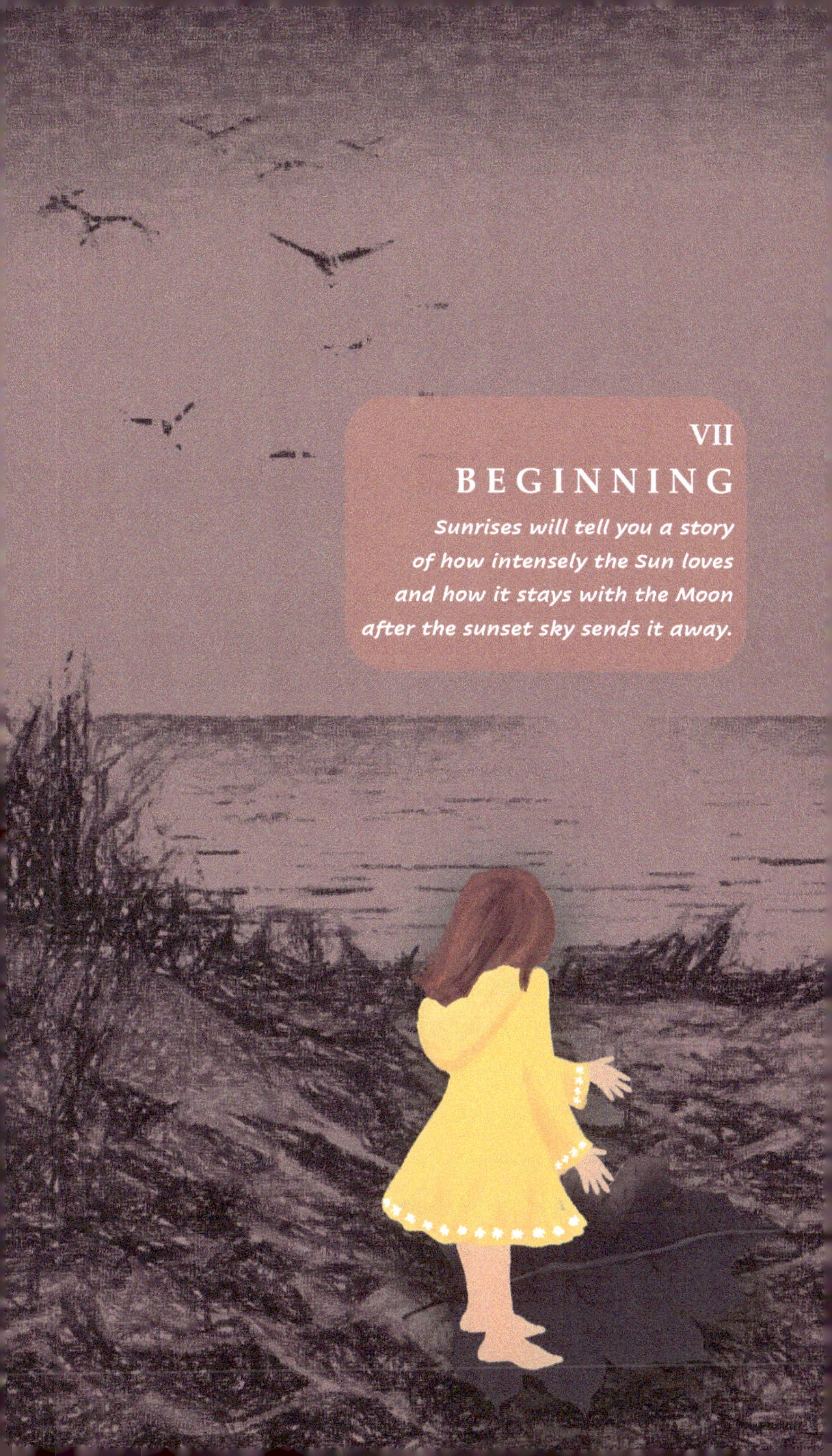

VII

BEGINNING

Sunrises will tell you a story
of how intensely the Sun loves
and how it stays with the Moon
after the sunset sky sends it away.

Who's Him?" I asked.

"The Creator", she answered,
her voice sliding over me
in a whisper.

Who's Him?" I asked.

This abject desire within me was new
as I noted the crown of thorns and bristles
and realized that those isolated branches
were arms stretched wide open,
in sacrifice for my wretchedness
so I could travel to this divine voice.

I felt myself being beckoned
by a voice so ethereally loving,
so radiantly magnificent,
full of splendor and brilliance,
that I no longer wished to stay
in the place I had fought to be in.

I started to sprint towards it
and the pain of my misery
felt like a dream
I no longer recalled.

Mother had taken me
through the agony of transforming
and Autumn's bare feet
had been the one
to release my story.

The Girl was a yellow lantern
of all the lessons I needed
to learn about love,
the way, the truth,
and the light.

Barefoot and falling, infinity is a number that has none to end

"Little Leaf?" Mother's voice,
echoed in the winds.

"I am home", I answered joyously
for I had already left.

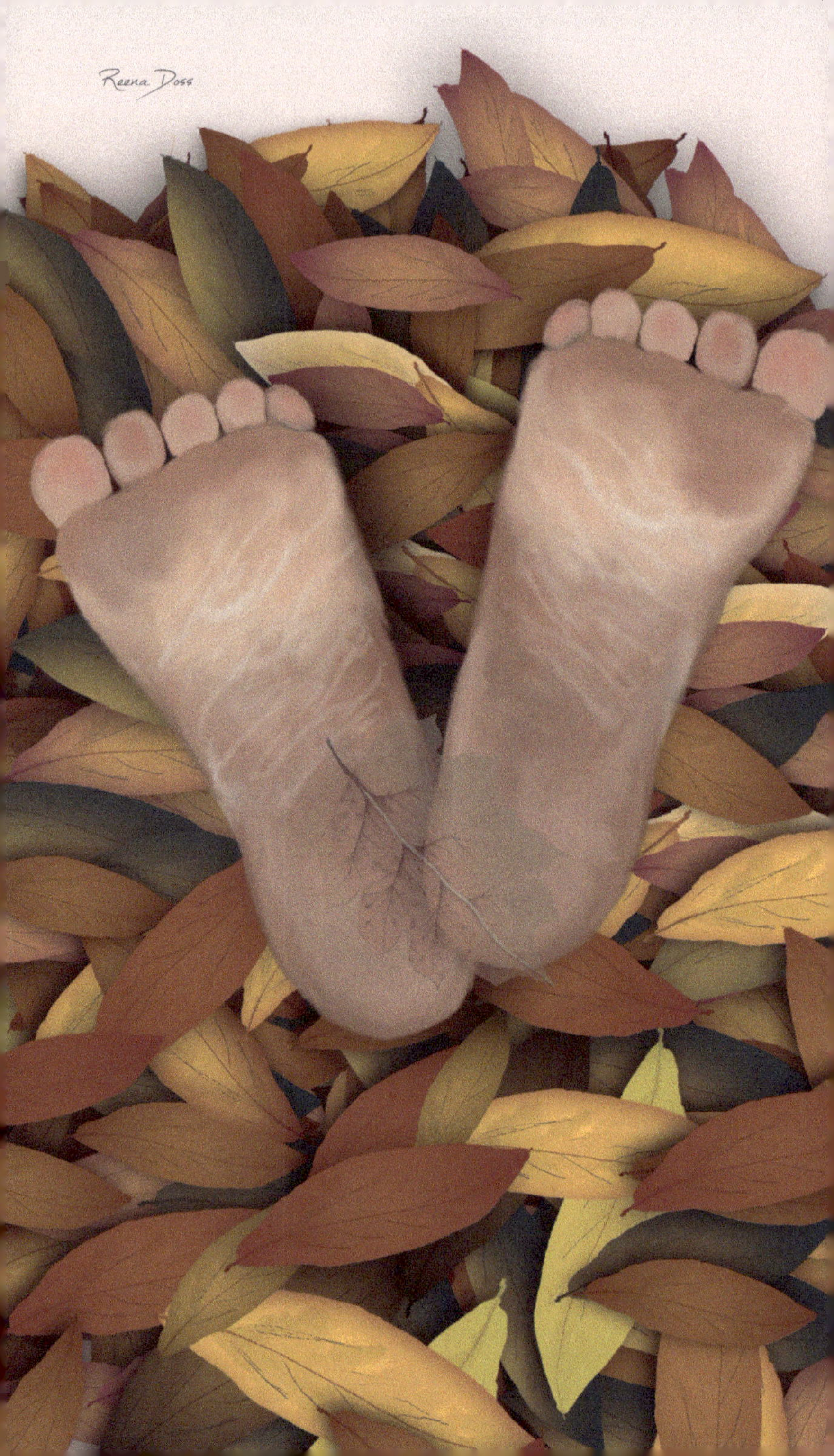
Reena Doss

Falling

I fall in abundance like the leaves do
for the carpet of flowers...
I see much about the headstrong winds
and how they dance in circles.

Embracing dreams after being heartbroken is for the boldest of hearts.

You fall into the new when you learn how to give up what is old and which no longer works in our life. Stagnancy is a deterrent for growth. It halts you on the journey of acceptance that what has past—happened, in order to give you the necessary tools to achieve happiness on the other side.

It takes a lot of grace to forgive yourself so that it can also be given to those who have done you an injustice. It takes a lot of courage to understand that your right to experience joy despite your mistakes and shortcomings is a gift that should never be taken for granted. It takes a lot of strength to slam into unconditional love, knowing that it will make your heart hurt as it expands to become an unlimited ocean with the stars in the sky, landing on Earth for the greatest adventure.

To leave the Earth in memory is a physical story about letting go of the mortal life for the immortal because death then becomes just another beginning to what is unseen but which the Weaver created as good... *so why then are we afraid of leaving unless we fear to accept the grace of worthiness that is freely given?*

Nature never tells a new generation the secret to living life here because she answers to the laws set by the Weaver who desires to develop a deep and personal relationship with you. And when you let Him, your heart will grow richer as His joy enters to show you the way. But He always lets you choose to discover Him.

In taking your first breath to the last, you breathe alone with the air that is His and freely given to you. That is why in this life, who else should be your best source of trust but in Him? In dating the Weaver, getting to know Him and His great love for you, you learn not to be afraid but to trust in His direction during the times when you cannot agree or see the ways in which He leads, teaches and guides you into the garden of eternity.

Always remember: Adversity never leaves you empty-handed. There will be plenty to harvest. Search and you will discover unimaginable treasure in every place that seemed to have taken the very best from you.

> *I am a part of it all, a rain storm of diamonds*
> *always sparkling like snowflakes on the tips of the trees.*

Barefoot and falling, infinity is a number that has none to end

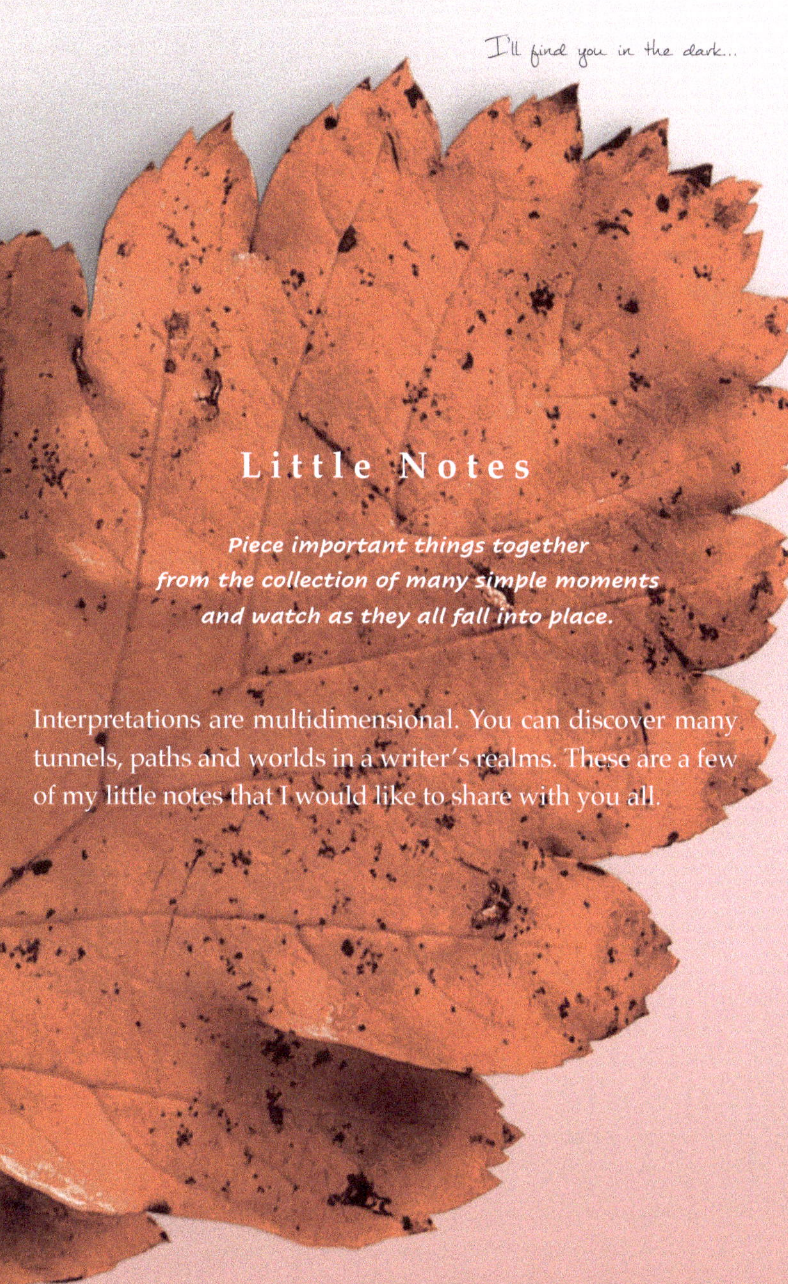

Little Notes

*Piece important things together
from the collection of many simple moments
and watch as they all fall into place.*

Interpretations are multidimensional. You can discover many
tunnels, paths and worlds in a writer's realms. These are a few
of my little notes that I would like to share with you all.

1. Themes

a) *Autumn*

Autumn is like fine wine that never grows old but gets better with time. If I could stay in a season, this would be it and yet paradoxically, Autumn is the season where I learn to let go. There is no particular way to describe home and yet nature teaches me exactly how to do this by embracing everything that other seasons keep giving—holding it all—and dropping away from my arms. In the end, what remains is what I keep. Autumn lightens everything heavy. The theme of Autumn connects the pages of my Indian skin like a golden thread in the range of the colors—*turquoise, emerald, teal, red, amber, russet and bronze*—that Fall falls under.

b) *Nature*

The notion of nature has mostly been focused on everything other than humans but I beg to differ. We are a part of nature yet we have been given the best job—*Gardeners*—though we have forgotten to teach the new generations how precious this is. Taking care of the Earth is important because it gives us a better, healthier and longer life here. I used the dark and light elements of nature—*i) in the introduction of children:* did you see the shadows in yourself that you harbor for the future of humanity as a whole? *ii) in the gentleness and strength of the Tree:* did you see how those who raise you play a part in teaching you through actions how to love yourself and others (with or without being able to interfere with life's hard lessons)? and *iii) in the calamities of storms, hurricanes and tsunamis:* did you see how you must travel to know your purpose (when you let go of what can no longer make you happy)?

Barefoot and falling, infinity is a number that has none to end

c) Purpose

The knowing of your purpose versus what you allow others to tell you what it is will often be the hardest obstacle you will have to conquer but when you do it, there is no going back because you will know exactly who you are and what you want to be for other people. We all want to pursue our passions so why do we allow those we expect to support us the most to influence, reject and condemn what we know is so very good? Very often, you will discover that *those who follow the path of their true essence will face obstacles* that have nothing to do with their gifts or voices but more about detaching from people who tell you they want the best for you but are actually advising you against your gifts based on their own stressors, concerns or disappointments. The gift given to you has the capacity to multiply into excess not just for you but for everyone in the world that needs it. This is why you must fight for it. Never give up. Take all the humiliation, the struggle and the pain that comes with pursuing what you were created to be. Sometimes, you will have support, sometimes, you will have judgment or criticism and most times, you will feel very alone. But that is okay. It is normal. When you chase after what is extraordinary, you will find what everyone else does. But when you do ordinary things like pursuing what you love to do (like something you may mistake for a hobby perhaps), you become extra-ordinary. This is because though you have been told by others that it is not enough to achieve in the world, your voice that is found from the broken oyster is *the pearl* that the world needs to bloom. This is why letting go of storm debris, toxicity and old protective layers formed over time is necessary to *embrace the passion, gifts and love you keep yourself from.*

2. Characters

b) Leaf:

The protagonist—the Leaf, will help you connect to the versions of yourself that found it hard to let go of false lens, old ideas and stagnant ways of living. A lifespan of a leaf is equal to the seasons. And its purpose though small, contributes to the bigger picture. Being who you are—*even if you are a leaf*—is no ordinary thing.

b) Girl

The Girl represents those who come to your aid whether they know it or not. In life, *you are never alone.* You feel this way when you keep looking for support and help at closed doors that never open themselves willingly to you no matter how much you knock on them. Sometimes, support comes in the form of angels disguised as humans and sometimes help comes in the form of adversity that takes on the shape of devastation, hardships and problems. Reflections of circumstances are not a bad thing—*for pausing and communicating with your lost self in a wild storm*—because they can reveal what is being destroyed to set you free.

c) Tree

The Tree represents the journey of death to life which is entered through the narrow gate in the crosses of your suffering (falling leaves) but freed in surrendering to the victorious one of Christ. The Leaf refers to the Tree as Mother (my connection to Our Lady) in how she helps her children find joy in surrender as she is intimately acquainted with *the human struggle to resist* this overpowering and overwhelming great love offered precisely at the time when you feel like you don't deserve it and which you will encounter in your greatest failures. When you let this love transform you, it ultimately leads us to peace in the end. The Leaf recognizes his journey's purpose when he realizes that his pride was a false illusion and actually stood in the way of everything that he wanted. How beautifully he lets go *to embrace his destiny.* This very act is what proves his humility (rather than him stating it) when he describes his emotions on entering the realm of forgiveness, grace and ever after, while at the same time respectfully calling the Tree—Mother.

3. Concepts

a) Bare feet

The digital painting of the Last Leaf on *the Girl's feet in the shape of a split heart* is a deliberate depiction of how all are connected through the Weaver's purpose, love for humanity and nature through imperfections, scars and the truth of who you are. No matter how much you run, or fly or swim, you come back to the land. It's like as if whatever mud is made up of, it is all beautifully transformed from the seeds that die to begin in the roots, from the roots that expand to grow into a trunk, from a trunk that stretches into branches and from branches that sprout leaves which birth stories before returning to honor the soil once again— *just like your body will one day rest for time in the garden of the Earth*—knowing that there will be more stories by others who will follow set paths to *find their own.*

b) Title

Leaves go through so much. I love to pause and contemplate the effective lessons that the Weaver teaches through His creations in nature. Everything the Weaver creates has a singular blueprint that can never be replicated—a grain of sand, a snowflake, a human thumbprint and a leaf. You are never repeated and never will be because the Weaver sees you as precious and infinite. Everything in nature sings of the Weaver's love for humanity, comforts with what lies in the unknown and tells you all you need to know about your purpose here and where you go after this short time on Earth. Life and death belong to Him and that's why everything is already covered under the grace of the Weaver. *The Last Leaf Of Autumn* is a title I chose because I wanted to explore the theme of death in a metaphorical, emotional and physical way and in this story, I was delighted to discover that if life begins at the end of death—whether it is a version of you that you don't yet know (metaphorical) or whether it is an internal one (emotional), then when your body can no longer survive with time (physical), you will be born into the eternal one. And thus, it suddenly became important *to tell the Leaf's story* about why you must make this life you've been given count.

c) Inspiration

There was a tree that stood outside my bedroom window. From the 1st floor, I loved watching it transform every season and I felt blessed to be able to learn its lessons. Many times when I have wanted to give up, this tree reminded me that change, growth and living were incredibly important, not because I was needed by those I wanted to need me but by those who I often didn't know yet. Maybe you take a lot for granted in life and when you don't feel seen by those you love, you do everything you can to make them see you until you learn that there is nothing you can do except surrender to the will of the Weaver who made you for the purpose that you exist. At first, it can be difficult to learn the truth of this. You may fight it, run from it and get into more hot water in your need to prove yourself right but in the end, you will understand that aligning with who you are born to be will automatically make you feel happy when life gets tough.

PS: For those wondering, I frequently refer to God as the Weaver or Creator as this is how I met Him as a little girl when looking at the stars one night. I knew He existed and I never questioned it even when I sometimes wondered during life's hardships if He may have forgotten me. That feeling though with the wind blowing wildly in the trees and fiercely all around me was not the same when it connected playfully with the knots in my hair. It was like the softest whisper, a gentle breeze that told me without any words needing to be said that I was loved by the one who made the stars, the moon and the space beyond the night sky that belonged to the Earth's gravity that kept me anchored. I remember yearning in that moment to run to Him but also knew that my time hadn't arrived.

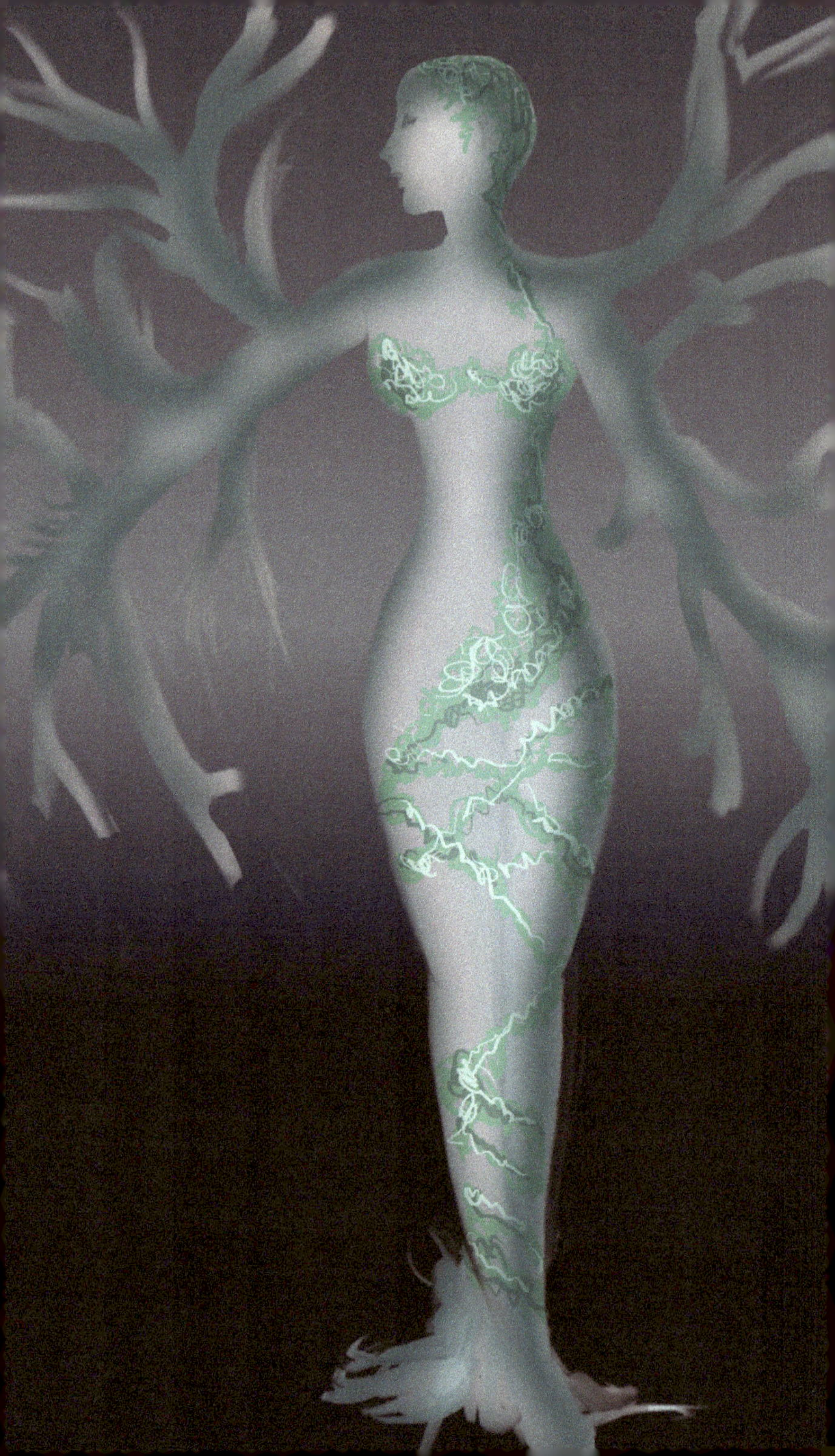

Acknowledgements
I am so grateful

Starting with my beloved Weaver, the love of my life to my loved ones: you all bring joy to my soul in ways I could never explain.

Quite simply, I love you all

When I thought I wasn't ready, the Weaver called me and I found myself saying, *"Yes"* without knowing the path in front of me. Nobody is prepared for this type of journey and the cost sometimes hit closer than I realized but I have never been the kind of person who avoided going into the unknown when I knew that Jesus was with me.

I took that inward journey with Him, with those I found ready to walk with me into the storms and I am so glad that I did. He gave me Mother Mary to comfort me often because He knew this journey would break me but it had to be done for the heart that sought him first in everything to be born. The Holy Spirit taught me how to use that gift of writing, art and creativity so now that I know my purpose, I realize how much I enjoy consulting Him. I cannot believe how I literally came to fear losing Him above anyone else. *Do you know how big that is?* I was once so terrified to lose the ones I loved until I lost them in a way that healed me.

While the same people can no longer control me through false perceptions of love, I also accept this as part of learning how to name, accept and embrace the deeper rooted crosses which are a victory.

It is good knowing I can start over towards my path as an author without any leftover questionable feelings of *"Am I on the right path?"* or being attached to the old ways. I feel, care and remember everything deeply and maybe this is why it has been more difficult for others to understand me. They see my expression as *"too much"* but one day, I hope we realize how beautifully unique we all are and why the Weaver added each one of us into this world—to give every human we meet exactly what they were hungry for, praying for or missing.

My beloved Weaver, *what would I do without you?* Thank you for always reminding me that the road is never over and if it was, there lies the ocean and there are still ships a-plenty. And should the ocean end and ships crash, there begins the sky and there are wings to fly far and wide right into adventures not known yet. And if the sky breaks open after the storms, clouds will part to reveal a universe that always awaits and yearns to be explored by hands that appreciate its unchartered worlds. Thank you for letting adversity use everyone I knew to bring out the real me you hid until ready to be seen.

My dearest family, I want you to know that I love you and I know that you love me too. How could we not? We are part of each other's roots. Thank you for all the memories that matter and which shaped me into who I choose to be today. I will not forget any of them easily.

Shruti, thank you for being my best friend, editor and for helping me through the darkest year I ever experienced in Gro. It is not something I could ever thank you for and I want to say here that I never take our 13+ years of friendship for granted because you are more sister to me than friend. You and your family have now become a part of my world too.

Miriam, you make the stars shine for me every day. You weave out magic, dust in dandelions and bring childlike wonder back into the forgotten realms of my inner worlds. Thank you for helping me develop this manuscript and the other, for never giving up—on me, my dreams and my beating heart that couldn't stop speaking in poetry, art and creativity every time we connected, collaborated or looked for clarity in each other.

Ismet, Suzana & Infinity, thank you for supporting me in practical ways throughout these years but especially when I wanted to give up. Thank you for listening to me whenever I couldn't sit with grief by myself. You sacrificed personal time every day to make space for quality time with me.

I got through a lot of the hard times because I could not help but realize how much love you poured into me. You are my precious wildflowers in a field of gold.

Darling LOML, there is in intangibility, tangible moments of great love not noticed at first when grief is all you feel, see and hear. Now there are lovely times that feel like soft ribbons I tie into bows when hope was sometimes difficult to feel. I keep you written in the fabric of my stories and the ones that are yet to be written but that live under my skin waiting to be told… This life is passing and I want to marry it with you before our time is up. You are the promise of my faith so how could I ever forget you from the yearning in my soul that screams out its gladness knowing that you exist? There are no words to describe how grateful I am for how love has wrapped my mind in a blanket of dreamy memories that I take with my heart everywhere I go. I hope the birds will carry my love—that I express in words, art and creativity—like silhouettes against the Moon so when you feel alone or feel far from my arms, their fluttering wings will help you remember how very loved you are by me.

Thank you, thank you, thank you!

Reena Doss

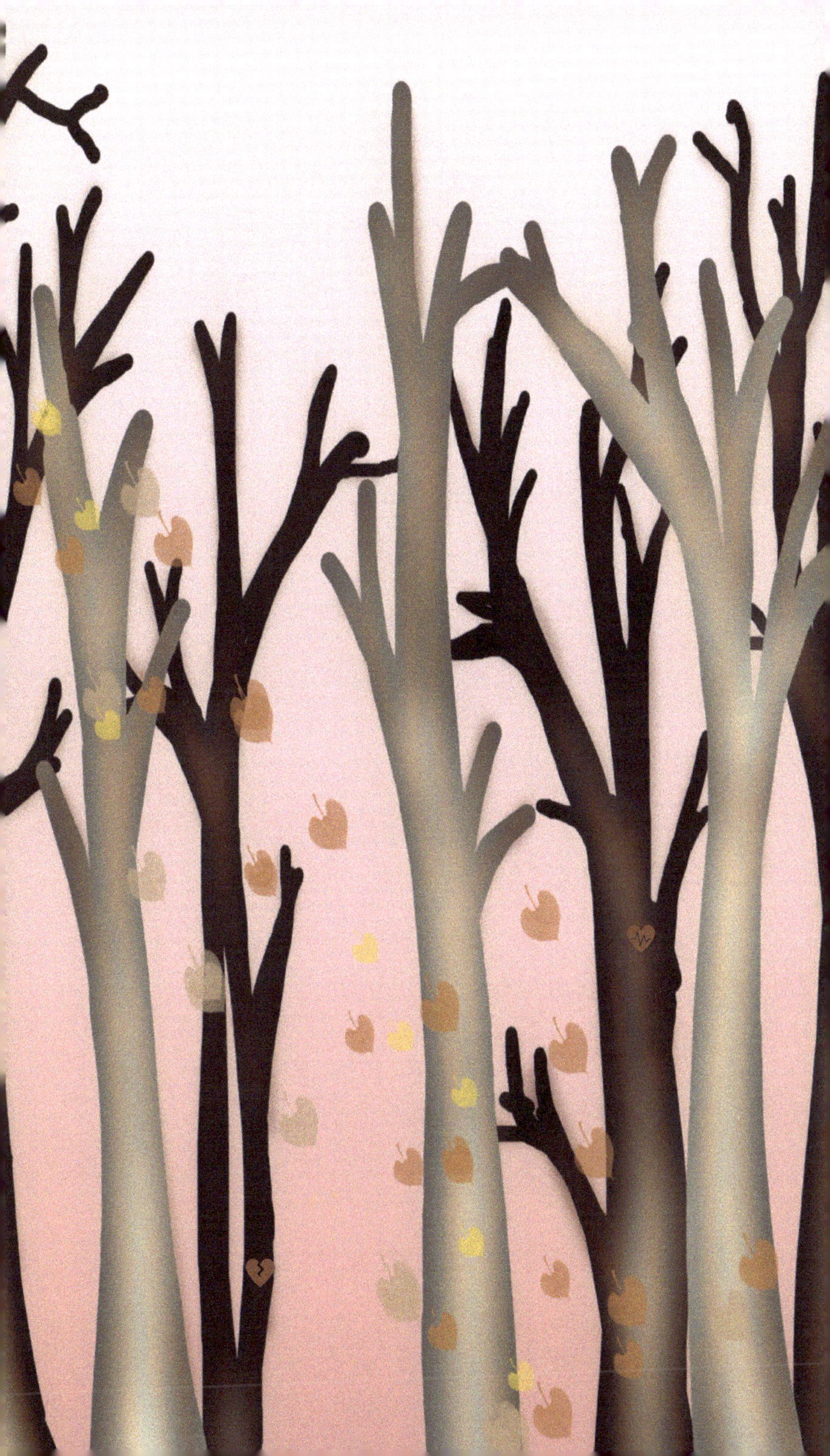

Reena Doss

About the Author

Reena Doss considers writing to be her first voice of expression, followed closely by art and creativity. Through the encouraging platform provided by the Instagram community, she reclaimed her lost voices, evolved a few others and discovered new ones along the way. This has redeemed her trust that consistent Hope, Faith and Love in what is true ignites what is impossible to occur. Her adoration for her beloved Weaver, the Celestial Sky, Nature and her fellow Earthians has given her immeasurable courage to endure every season with a resilience born from battles overcome.

Born in Calcutta with roots drawn from Chennai and Pondicherry, Reena Doss has lived most of her life in the south of India—Bangalore. Though she prefers traveling to far-off places inside her head, she sometimes ventures into the world that others call real.

You can try and catch her but it may not always be possible as she is generally off on adventures flying on phoenix wings, swimming into the deep with mermaids and chasing fiery dragons down for stories.

> *To those who remain true to themselves*
> *to those who create magic wherever they go*
> *and for those who sit beside the hurt*
> *when everyone else leaves,*
> *Art will always immortalize you.*

Please scan the following QR code to follow her
on Instagram @reenadossauthor

www.reenadoss.com

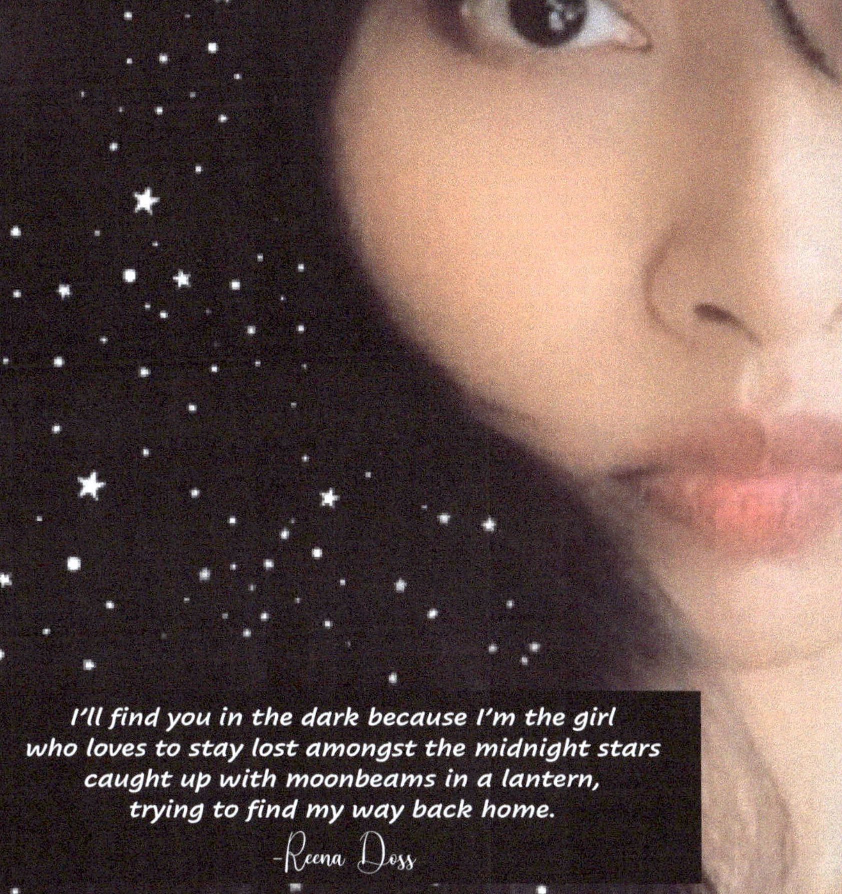
I'll find you in the dark because I'm the girl
who loves to stay lost amongst the midnight stars
caught up with moonbeams in a lantern,
trying to find my way back home.

-Reena Doss

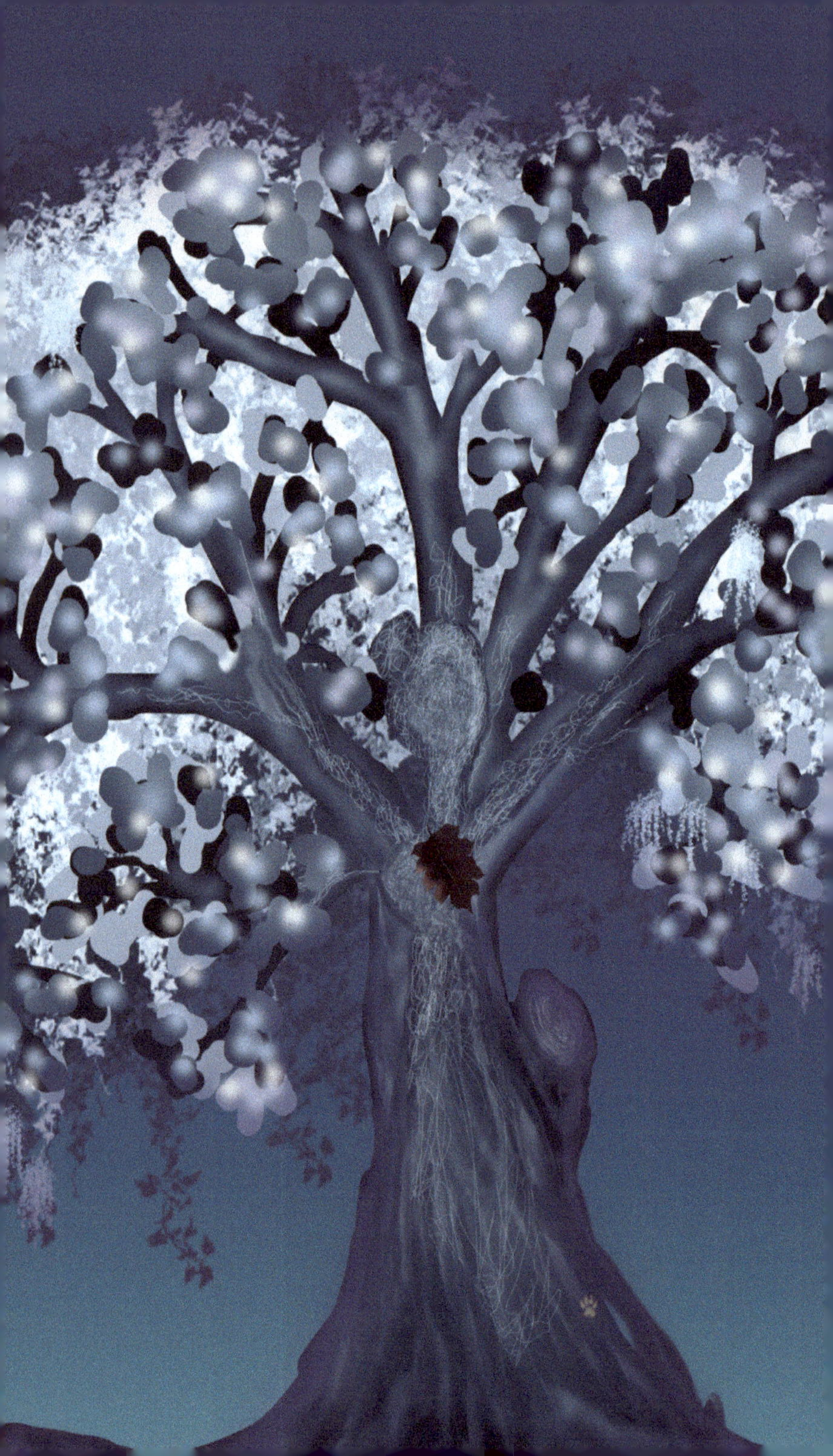

Ink Gladiators Press®

Publishing and promoting warriors on life's battlefield

We serve the community of creatives as a whole. We love to publish, promote and preserve the voices of authors, writers, artists, poets, lyricists, photographers, philosophers, editors, designers, storytellers, mental health advocates, communities and creators.

Our aim is focused on a vision where authors, professionals and creatives can grow together by contributing their heart songs to humanity as gifts of inspiration where reality can be built through the art of dream-making. We look forward to welcoming your voices, their expressions and inviting them to make a home with our Ink Gladiator family through our anthologies, workshops and other supportive avenues. Not only do we offer A Hand To Hold Publishing where we recommend professional freelancers to help you on your publishing path, we also review and recommend publications that we enjoy reading so feel free to email us about your books before sending them to us in the format you are most comfortable with.

When we work together with faith, hope and love, everything is possible. We appreciate your love for reading and for being a part of our journey! Thank you for being here.

For any inquiries, please email us at contact@inkgladiatorspress.com.

We remain at your service,
Ink Gladiators Press® Team
www.inkgladiatorspress.com

*Please scan the QR Code below to follow us
on Instagram @inkgladiatorspress*

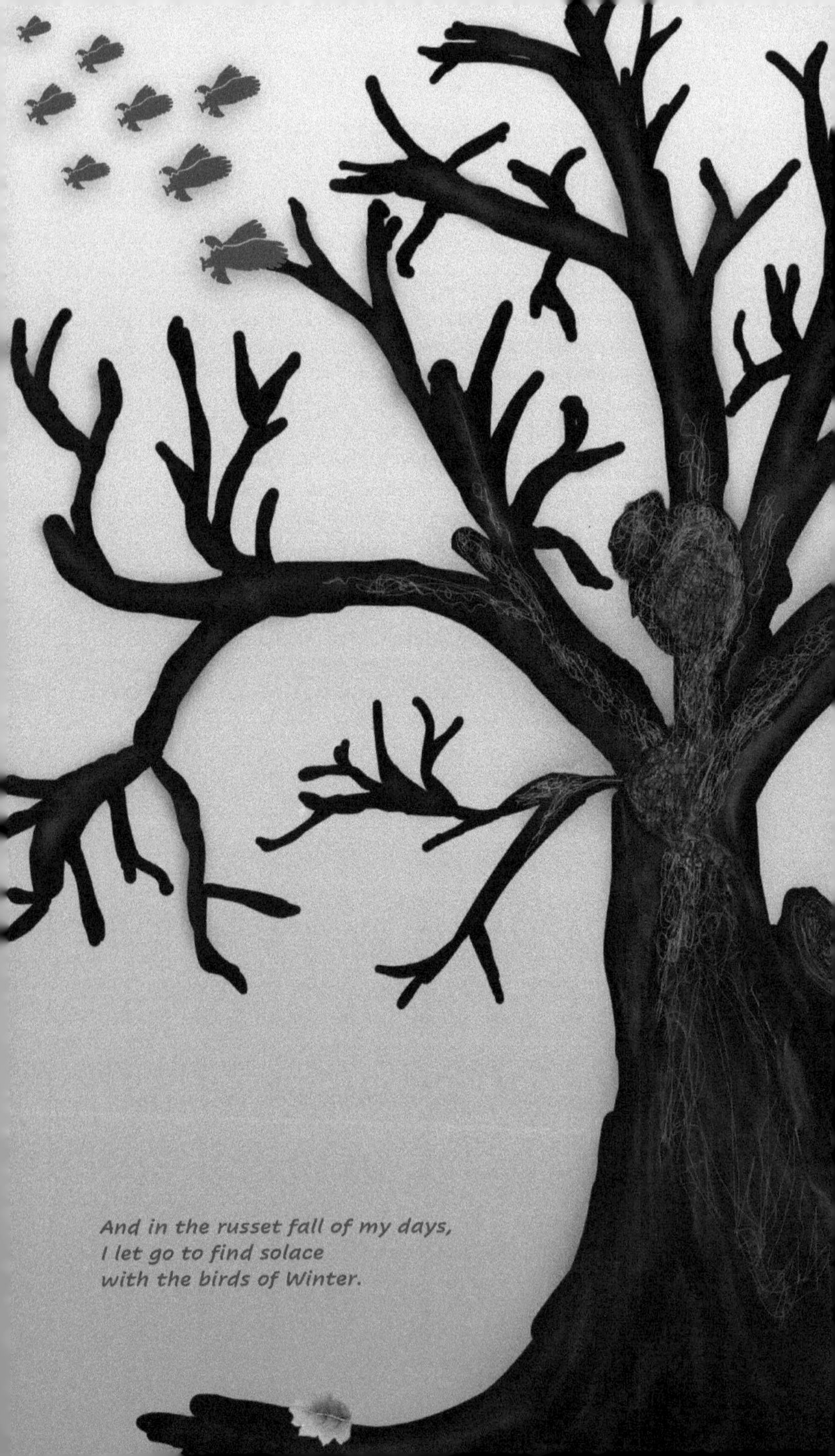
And in the russet fall of my days,
I let go to find solace
with the birds of Winter.